Math Basics

T0011756

Shapes Everywhere

By Nick Rebman

level
1
little blue
readers

www.littlebluehousebooks.com

Little Blue House is distributed by North Star Editions:
sales@northstareditions.com | 888-417-0195

Produced for Little Blue House by Red Line Editorial.

Photographs ©: Shutterstock Images, cover, 4, 7, 9, 11, 12–13, 15, 16 (top left), 16 (top right), 16 (bottom left), 16 (bottom right)

Library of Congress Control Number: 2020900852

ISBN
978-1-64619-169-7 (hardcover)
978-1-64619-203-8 (paperback)
978-1-64619-271-7 (ebook pdf)
978-1-64619-237-3 (hosted ebook)

Printed in the United States of America
Mankato, MN
012021

About the Author

Nick Rebman enjoys reading, walking his dog, and traveling to places where he doesn't speak the language. He lives in Minnesota.

Table of Contents

Shapes Everywhere

I see a circle.

I see a square.

I see a triangle.

I see a rectangle.

rectangle

I see a star.

I see a heart.

heart

Glossary

heart

star

rectangle

triangle

Index